CW00549085

1,000,000 Books

are available to read at

www.ForgottenBooks.com

Read online
Download PDF
Purchase in print

ISBN 978-1-5280-2854-7
PIBN 10895565

This book is a reproduction of an important historical work. Forgotten Books uses
state-of-the-art technology to digitally reconstruct the work, preserving the original format
whilst repairing imperfections present in the aged copy. In rare cases, an imperfection in
the original, such as a blemish or missing page, may be replicated in our edition. We do,
however, repair the vast majority of imperfections successfully; any imperfections that
remain are intentionally left to preserve the state of such historical works.

Forgotten Books is a registered trademark of FB &c Ltd.
Copyright © 2018 FB &c Ltd.
FB &c Ltd, Dalton House, 60 Windsor Avenue, London, SW19 2RR.
Company number 08720141. Registered in England and Wales.

For support please visit www.forgottenbooks.com

1 MONTH OF
FREE
READING

at

www.ForgottenBooks.com

By purchasing this book you are eligible for one month membership to ForgottenBooks.com, giving you unlimited access to our entire collection of over 1,000,000 titles via our web site and mobile apps.

To claim your free month visit: www.forgottenbooks.com/free895565

* Offer is valid for 45 days from date of purchase. Terms and conditions apply.

English
Français
Deutsche
Italiano
Español
Português

www.forgottenbooks.com

Mythology Photography **Fiction**
Fishing Christianity **Art** Cooking
Essays Buddhism Freemasonry
Medicine **Biology** Music **Ancient
Egypt** Evolution Carpentry Physics
Dance Geology **Mathematics** Fitness
Shakespeare **Folklore** Yoga Marketing
Confidence Immortality Biographies
Poetry **Psychology** Witchcraft
Electronics Chemistry History **Law**
Accounting **Philosophy** Anthropology
Alchemy Drama Quantum Mechanics
Atheism Sexual Health **Ancient History**
Entrepreneurship Languages Sport
Paleontology Needlework Islam
Metaphysics Investment Archaeology
Parenting Statistics Criminology
Motivational

ANNUAL REPORT

OF THE

DEPARTMENT OF POLICE

OF THE

CITY OF BUFFALO
NEW YORK

For the Year Ending
December 31, 1928

NATIONAL INSTITUTE OF PUBLIC ADMINISTRATION
BUREAU OF MUNICIPAL RESEARCH
261 BROADWAY,   NEW YORK CITY

HV

The Chief Executives of the Buffalo Police Department

Since its formation as a uniformed force in the year 1866, giving dates and duration of their service.

		Yrs.	Mos.	Days
Supt. David Reynolds*	May 7, 1866—March 6, 1870	3	9	29
Supt. Peter C. Doyle*	April 1, 1870—May 1, 1872	2	1	0
Supt. John Byrne*	May 1, 1872—May 26, 1879	7	0	25
Supt. William A. Phillips*	May 26, 1879—Jan. 14, 1880	0	7	18
Supt. William J. Wolf*	Jan. 14, 1880—Dec. 28, 1882	2	11	14
Supt. James H. Shepard*	Dec. 28, 1882—May 12, 1883	0	4	14
Supt. Thomas Curtin*	May 12, 1883—July 31, 1884	1	2	19
Supt. William A. Phillips*	July 31, 1884—Mar. 18, 1887	2	7	17
Supt. Martin Morin*	Mar. 18, 1887—Jan. 22, 1891	3	10	4
Supt. Daniel Morgenstern*	Jan. 22, 1891—June 1, 1893	2	4	9
Supt. George Chambers*	June 1, 1893—March 7, 1894	0	9	6
Supt. William S. Bull*	March 7, 1894—Jan. 24, 1906	11	10	17
Act. Supt. John Martin	Jan. 24, 1906—April 23, 1906	0	3	29
Supt. Michael Regan*	April 23, 1906—Dec. 24, 1915	9	8	1
Chief John Martin	Jan. 1, 1916—Jan. 2, 1918	2	0	1
Chief Henry J. Girvin	Jan. 2, 1918—May 1, 1919	1	3	29
Acting Chief James W. Higgins	Feb. 18, 1919—May 1, 1919	0	2	13
Chief James W. Higgins	May 1, 1919—Jan. 1, 1922	2	8	0
Chief John F. Burfeind*	Jan. 2, 1922—Dec. 31, 1923	1	11	29
Chief Charles F. Zimmerman	Jan. 1, 1924—March 31, 1926	2	3	0
Acting Chief James W. Higgins	Jan. 1, 1926—March 31, 1926	0	3	0
Chief James W. Higgins	April 1, 1926—Dec. 31, 1927	1	9	0
Commissioner James W. Higgins	January 1, 1928—			

*Deceased.

ANNUAL REPORT

Office of Commissioner of Police

To The Honorable Mayor
and Common Council,
Buffalo, N. Y.

January 1, 1929

Gentlemen:—

Herewith please find the Fifty-fifth Annual Report of the Buffalo Police Department, for the year ending December 31, 1928, and the first Annual Report under the new Charter. An effort has been made to conform to the standard for Annual Reports as outlined by the Committee on Uniform Crime Records of the International Association of Chiefs of Police.

One of the outstanding features in the development of the department during the year was the introduction of radio into police service. A beginning was made on February 9, 1928, broadcasting police news items from Police Headquarters through Station WEBR. Reports of missing persons, warnings of the operation of criminals, and descriptions of stolen automobiles are broadcast daily at 11 o'clock A.M. Am pleased to announce that the application of the radio to police work has demonstrated ·that it can be made a wonderful adjunct to the system of communication now in use. The experience we have had during the past months forecasts much greater accomplishment with a station built by the city and operated entirely as a police unit, which will make possible broadcasting to moving police automobiles. It is hoped that this station will be constructed and in operation during the coming year.

A movement was begun early in 1928 to interest the heads of other police departments in the establishment of a uniform report system for stolen automobiles; the need of something of this kind being apparent for some years. Owing to the common use of such vehicles by criminals, affording them wide range and favorable odds for escape after a serious crime, it was believed that its adoption would in a measure help to curb the activities of this class by keeping the local police informed in this respect. The Buffalo Police have always made good use of such information and the many important arrests made for other departments supports our theory. A number of department heads believed the scheme worthy of a trial and co-operated by adopting a standard report card size 3x5 which is used for exchanging stolen car information and has an advantage over the old method because no additional labor is necessary to prepare the information for filing.

The flash light system is being extended and when the work under the present contract is completed, the system will be in service in all but four of the seventeen police precincts. Added protection will be given the residents of the districts by establishing a quick form of communication from station house to man on post. Signals flashed from the station house are answered in a very short time and the patrolman is thus made acquainted with the details of any matter requiring attention.

The various statistical tables included in this report, contain data with respect to the prevelancy of crime in this community. A gratifying decrease in major crimes with the exception of robbery is noted; this offense shows an increase of fifteen over the preceeding year. A total of 41,684 arrests were made during the year, 2694 being for major offenses.

The situation as regards vice and gambling, on the whole, is very satisfactory. Constant effort is being made by the department to suppress commercialized vice in all its forms and I feel we have succeeded to a great extent.

The appropriation for the department for the fiscal year ending July 1, 1929, amounts to $3,172,968.82 plus $42,000 allowed for Automobile maintenance.

The program of action for the ensuing year for which the necessary funds have been made available provides for the development of the Police Radio System for broadcasting to moving police automobiles.

To further promote the efficiency of the department the following recommendations are offered:

That the flash light system be extended to include the remaining four police precincts, giving us a city-wide flashlight system.

That a modern, fireproof building be constructed for Police Headquarters, to replace the present structure built in 1884. The development of the different bureaus housed there is retarded because of lack of room and proper facilities.

To insure better supervision and give added protection, I sincerely urge that an additional six captains and two hundred patrolmen be appointed to the present Force.

In conclusion, I wish to express to the Honorable Mayor and Common Council my sincere thanks for the co-operation extended to the department during the past year.

Sincerely yours,

JAMES W. HIGGINS,
Commissioner.

Department of Police

James W. Higgins
Commissioner

John S. Marnon
Deputy Commissioner

Frank J. Carr
Deputy Commissioner

Thomas J. Gilligan
Inspector

James Hyland
Inspector

John G. Reville
Chief of Detectives

Emanuel Schuh, Assistant Chief of Detectives.
Thomas J. Riordan, Assistant Chief of Detectives.
Edwin A. Bowerman, Surgeon.
Victor A. Tyrasinski, Assistant Surgeon.
George A. Schmidt, Chief Desk Lieutenant.
Thomas Coyle, Assistant Chief Desk Lieutenant.
John E. Regan, Clerk to the Chief of Police.
Joseph T. Whitwell, Chief of the Bertillion System.
James Connors, Assistant Chief of the Bertillion System.
Reinhold Schulz, Photographer.
Henry W. Alt, Supt. of Motive Power and Supplies.
Leo Rowland, Chief of the Police Signal System.
William B. Fairbairn, Asst. Chief of the Police Signal System.
William Hildebrand, Clerk (Bureau) and Property Clerk.
Jacob J. Gaiser, Stenographer.

POLICE HEADQUARTERS
Corner Seneca and Franklin Streets

James W. Higgins, Commissioner

Commissioner of Police 1
Deputy Commissioners of Police 2
Inspectors 2
Surgeon 1
Assistant Surgeon 1
Captains 2
Chief Desk Lieutenant 1
Assistant Chief Desk Lieutenant 1
Chief of Traffic 1
Clerk (Bureau) And Property Clerk 1
Desk Lieutenants, divers duties 24
Lieutenants 3
Superintendent of Motive Power and Supplies 1
Patrolmen, assigned to divers duties 95

Total 136

DETECTIVE BUREAU
Police Headquarters
Seneca and Franklin Streets

John G. Reville, Chief of Detectives

Chief of Detectives 1
Assistant Chief of Detectives 2
Lieutenants 2
Desk Lieutenants 2
Detective Sergeants 44
Detectives 22
Patrolmen 14
Policewomen 4

Total 91

Precinct Boundaries

FIRST PRECINCT
Station House, Seneca and Franklin Streets

The First Precinct embraces the territory within the following described boundaries: South Michigan and Michigan Avenue to Eagle Street, to Niagara Street, to Virginia Street, and a continuation thereof, westerly to its intersection with the westerly line of the State of New York, thence southerly and easterly along said State Line to its intersection with the southerly continuation of South Michigan Avenue.

SECOND PRECINCT
Station House, 500 South Division Street

The Second Precinct embraces the territory within the following described boundaries:' Michigan Avenue from the site of the old Hamburg Canal to Clinton Street, to Fillmore Avenue, to Smith Street, to Perry Street, to Hamburg Street, to the site of the old Hamburg Canal to Michigan Avenue.

THIRD PRECINCT
Station House, Washington and Tupper Streets

The Third Precinct embraces the territory within the following described boundaries: Niagara Street from Eagle Street, to Virginia Street, to Elmwood Avenue, to North Street, to Michigan Avenue, to Eagle Street, to Niagara Street.

FOURTH PRECINCT
Station House, Sycamore and Ash Streets

The Fourth Precinct embraces the territory within the following described boundaries: Michigan Avenue from Clinton Street, to North Street, to Jefferson Avenue, to Clinton Street, to Michigan Avenue.

FIFTH PRECINCT
Station House, Delavan Avenue and Greenwood Place

The Fifth Precinct embraces the territory within the following described boundaries: Elmwood Avenue from West Utica Street to the center line of Scajaquada Creek, along the said center line and the westerly continuation thereof to the westerly line of the State of New York, southerly along said line to the intersection with the westerly continuation of the center of Massachusetts Avenue, to Front Avenue, to Rhode Island Street, to West Utica Street, to Elmwood Avenue.

SIXTH PRECINCT
Station House, 1444 Main Street

The Sixth Precinct embraces the territory within the following described boundaries: North Street from Elmwood Avenue to Jefferson Avenue, to Best Street, to Roehrer Avenue, to East Ferry Street, to Humboldt Parkway, to East Delavan Avenue, to Fillmore Avenue, to Kensington Avenue, to Humboldt Parkway, to Agassiz Place, to Delaware Park, along southern line to Delaware Park, to Delaware Avenue, to Rumsey Road, to Lincoln Parkway, to south line of Delaware Park, Penhurst Park to Penhurst Place, to Elmwood Avenue, to North Street.

SEVENTH PRECINCT
Station House, 355 Louisiana Street

The Seventh Precinct embraces the territory within the following described boundaries: South Michigan Avenue and Michigan Avenue to the site of the old Hamburg Canal to Hamburg Street, to Perry Street, to Smith Street, to Buffalo River to the N.Y.C.R.R. tracks to the City Line and westerly continuation thereof, to its intersection with the southerly line of the State of New York, westerly along said line to its intersection with the southerly continuation of the center line of South Michigan Avenue.

EIGHTH PRECINCT
Station House, 647 Fillmore Avenue

The Eighth Precinct embraces the territory within the following described boundaries: Clinton Street, from Jefferson Avenue to the Junction of Babcock Street west of the Erie R.R. tracks, northerly along Babcock Street to William Street, thence north to the N.Y.C.R.R. "Y" to Newton Street, along the westerly line of the N.Y.C.R.R. Belt Line to Sycamore Street, to Jefferson Avenue to Clinton Street.

NINTH PRECINCT
Station House, Seneca and Babcock Streets

The Ninth Precinct embraces the territory within the following described boundaries: Clinton Street from the City Line to Bailey Avenue, to the junction of Dingens Street, thence westerly along the center line of Dingens Street to its intersection with Babcock Street, along Babcock Street west of the Erie R.R. tracks to Clinton Street, to Fillmore Avenue, to Smith Street, to the Buffalo River, thence easterly along Buffalo River to Cazenovia Creek, to Cazenovia Street to Abbott Road. Thence along Abbott Road and Potter Road to the southeasterly boundary of Cazenovia Park, northeasterly along this boundary to Cazenovia Creek, easterly along the Creek to the City Line, thence along the City Line to Clinton Street, the place of beginning.

TENTH PRECINCT
Station House, 566 Niagara Street

The Tenth Precinct embraces the territory within the following described boundaries: Virginia Street from the river front to Elmwood Avenue, to West Utica Street, to Rhode Island Street, to Front Avenue, to Massachusetts Avenue, to the westerly line of the State of New York along said line to its intersection with the continuation of the westerly line of Virginia Street.

ELEVENTH PRECINCT
Station House, Broadway and Bailey Avenue

The Eleventh Precinct embraces the territory within the following described boundaries: Clinton Street from the City Line to Bailey Avenue, to the junction of Dingens Street, westerly along the continuation of the center line of Dingens Street to its intersection with Babcock Street, to William Street, thence directly north to the N.Y.C.R.R. "Y" to Newton Street, along the westerly line of the N.Y.C.R.R. Belt Line tracks to Sycamore Street, to Walden Avenue, to the City Line, to Clinton Street.

TWELFTH PRECINCT
Station House, 1186 Genesee Street

The Twelfth Precinct embraces the territory within the following described boundaries: Walden Avenue from the City Line to Sycamore Street, to Jefferson Avenue, to Best Street, to Roehrer Avenue, to East Ferry Street, to Humboldt Parkway, to East Delavan Avenue, to Grider Street, to East Ferry Street, to Bailey Avenue, to Genesee Street, to City Line and southerly along said City Line to Walden Avenue and the place of beginning.

THIRTEENTH PRECINCT
Station House, Austin Street and Josyln Place

The Thirteenth Precinct embraces the territory within the following described boundaries: Elmwood Avenue City Line to the center line of Scajaquada Creek, along said center line and a continuation thereof to its intersection with the westerly line of the State of New York, along said State Line to its intersection with the westerly continuation of the City Line, along said City Line to Elmwood Avenue.

FOURTEENTH PRECINCT
Station House, 2895 Main Street

The Fourteenth Precinct embraces the territory within the following described boundaries: East Delavan Avenue from Fillmore to Grider Street, to Kensington Avenue, to the Erie R.R. tracks, to Amherst Street, to Parkridge Avenue, to Winspear, to Bailey, to Main Street, southwest along Main Street to Kenmore Avenue, to Starin Avenue, to Amherst Street, to Parkside Avenue, to Agassiz Place, to Humboldt Parkway, to Kensington Avenue, to Fillmore Avenue, to East Delavan Avenue and the point of beginning.

FIFTEENTH PRECINCT
Station House, Whitfield and South Park Avenue

The Fifteenth Precinct embraces the territory within the following described boundaries: ommencing at Smith Street and the Buffalo River, following the southerly course of the Buff- lo River to its junction with Cazenovia Creek, thence along Cazenovia Creek to Cazenovia treet, south along Cazenovia Street, to Abbott Road, southeasterly along Abbott and Potter oad to the southeasterly boundary of Cazenovia Park, thence northerly to Cazenovia Creek, hence easterly to the City Line and south along the City Line to the N.Y.C. R.R. tracks, thence long the said tracks to the Buffalo River, thence along the Buffalo River to Smith Street, the ılace of beginning.

SIXTEENTH PRECINCT
Station House, Bailey and Collingwood Avenue

The Sixteenth Precinct embraces the territory within the following described boundaries: ommencing at Grider Street and East Ferry Street, east to Bailey Avenue, to Genesee Street,) easterly City Line, northerly along the City Line and easterly continuation thereof to Bailey venue, to Winspear Avenue, to Parkridge Avenue, to Amherst Street, to Delaware, Lacka- anna and Western R.R. tracks, southerly along the east side of railroad bank to Kensington venue, thence to Grider Street, to East Ferry Street, the place of beginning.

SEVENTEENTH PRECINCT
Station House, Colvin and Linden Avenue

The Seventeenth Precinct embraces the territory within the following described boundar- ˙es: Starin Avenue City Line to Amherst Street, to Nottingham Terrace, to Elmwood Avenue, to City Line, along the City Line to Starin Avenue, the point of beginning.

SUB-SEVENTEENTH PRECINCT
Station House, Delaware Park, near the Boat House

The Sub-Seventeenth Precinct embraces the territory within the following described boundaries: Nottingham Terrace to Amherst, to Parkside, to the south side of Delaware Park, to Rumsey Road, to Lincoln Parkway, south line of Delaware Park to Elmwood Avenue, to Nottingham Terrace, the point of beginning.

11

TABLE I

Personnel, Salary Scale, and Distribution of the Police Department: December 31, 1928.

FORCE

No.	Ranks and Grades	Annual Salary Scale, Dollars	1	2	3	4	5	6	7	8	9	10	11	12	13	14	15	16	17	Sub. 17	H.D.	Det. Bur.	Traf. Div.	Rel'v'g Capts.	Auto Sq.	Gar.
1	Commissioner	5,800																			1					
1	Dep. Commissioner	4,300																			1					
1	Dep. Commissioner	3,800																			1					
1	Chief of Detectives	3,800																				1				
2	Inspectors	3,800																			2					
2	Asst. Chief of Detectives	3,030																				2				
1	Chief Desk Lieutenant	3,030																			1					
1	Asst. Chief Desk Lieutenant	2,550																			1					
1	Clerk (Bur.) & Prop. Clerk	3,030																			1					
1	Supt. Motor Power & Supplies	3,000																			1					
1	Asst. Chief Bertillion System	2,730																				1				
1	Surgeon	3,060																			1					
1	Asst. Surgeon	2,400																			1					
29	Captains*	3,030	1	1	2	1	1	1	1	1	1	1	1	1	1	1	1	1	1	1				10		
2	Captains	2,790																					2			
1	Chief of Traffic	2,730																					1			
1	Chief Park Patrolman	2,550																			1					
65	Lieutenants	2,550	5	4	10	5	3	3	3	4	2	3	2	3	3	3	3	3	3	1			1		1	
5	Lieutenants	2,490						1			1		1										1		1	
41	Detective Sergeants	2,490																				41				
3	Detective Sergeants	2,370																				3				
75	Detectives	2,370	5	3	4	4	3	3	2	5	2	4	3	3	3	2	2	2	2		1	10			12	
78	Desk Lieutenants	2,370	3	3	3	3	3	3	3	3	3	3	3	3	3	3	3	3	3	2	22	2	1			
1	Desk Lieutenant	2,250																			1					
807	Patrolmen	2,250	97	33	80	37	31	40	31	55	37	31	30	43	39	29	31	22	19	12	47	11	48		3	1
45	Patrolmen	1,950	1	2	5	4	3	3		4	2	3	1	3	3	1	2	3	5							
4	Policewomen	2,100																				4				
5	Matrons	1,800		5																						
1177	Total		112	51	104	54	44	54	40	72	48	45	41	56	52	39	42	34	33	16	83	75	54	10	17	1

*10 Captains were employed relieving the Captains in all precincts, for their weekly vacations, excepting the Third Precinct.

NOTE: The salaries of the following officers were increased for the year 1929 as follows: The Commissioner to $7,000; the Deputy Commissioners to $5,000 and the Chief of Detectives to $4,500.

TABLE I-A

Personnel, Salary Scale, and Distribution of the Police Department; December 31, 1928.

CIVILIANS

No.	Grades	Annual Salary Dollars	1	2	3	4	5	6	7	8	9	10	11	12	13	14	15	16	17	Sub. 17	H.D.	Elec. Bur.	Traf. Div.	Garage
1	Clerk to Chief	3,030																			1			
1	Stenographer	2,760																			1			
1	Chief Bertillion System	3,000																			1	1		
1	Chief Police Signal System	3,300																				1		
1	Asst. Chief Police Sig. Sys.	2,850																				1		
1	Switchboardman	2,340																				1		
1	Cable Splicer ($6.50 per day)																					1		
1	Cable Splicer Helper ($5.33 per day)	2,490																				1		
1	Construction Foreman	2,370																				1		
1	Instrument Man	2,250																				1		
1	Asst. Instrument Repairer	2,370																				1		
1	Batteryman	2,250																				1		
15	Linemen	2,850																				15		
1	Foreman Mechanical Div.	2,100																						1
10	Mechanic's Assistants	2,370																						10
14	Mechanic's Helpers	2,490																						12
1	Asst. Marine Engineer	3,100	1																					
1	Photographer	2,100																			1			
1	Janitor #1 Stn. & H.D.	1,620																			1			
16	Janitors	2,250		1	1	1	1	1	1	1	1	1	1	1	1	1	1	1	1					
1	Janitresses	2,400	1																					
1	Woodworking Machinist	1,950	1																					
1	Tool Dresser																							1
1	Millwright	2,100																						1
1	Porter																						1	
1	Stableman ($5.50 per day)																							1
38	Laborers ($5.00 per day)																					7	5	21
1	Watchman (Charles St.)	2,100	1																					
119	**Total**		**9**	**2**	**2**	**1**	**1**	**1**	**1**	**1**	**1**	**1**	**1**	**1**	**1**	**1**	**2**	**1**	**2**		**5**	**31**	**6**	**48**

13

TABLE II

Changes in Authorized and Actual Strength of Police Department

RANKS and GRADES	AUTHORIZED STRENGTH Jan. 1	AUTHORIZED STRENGTH Dec. 31	ACTUAL STRENGTH Jan. 1	ACTUAL STRENGTH Dec. 31	Net Gain or Loss
Commissioner	1	1	1	1	—
Deputy Commissioners	2	2	2	2	—
Chief of Detectives	1	1	1	1	—
Asst. Chiefs of Detectives	2	2	2	2	—
Inspectors	2	2	2	2	—
Chief Desk Lieutenant	1	1	1	1	—
Asst. Chief Desk Lieutenant	1	1	1	1	—
Clerk (Bur.) & Prop. Clerk	1	1	1	1	—
Supt. Motor Power & Supplies	1	1	1	1	—
Asst. Chief Bertillion System	1	1	1	1	—
Surgeon	1	1	1	1	—
Asst. Surgeon	1	1	1	1	—
Captains	31	31	30	31	+
Chief of Traffic	1	1	1	1	—
Chief Park Patrolmen	1	1	1	1	—
Lieutenants	70	70	70	70	—
Detective Sergeants	44	44	44	44	—
Detectives	75	75	75	75	—
Desk Lieutenants	79	79	79	79	—
Patrolmen	852	852	852	852	—
Policewomen	4	4	4	4	—
Matrons	5	5	5	5	—
	1177	1177	1176	1177	+1

TABLE II-A

Daily Average Strength of Patrol Force

1. Total number of patrolmen 852
2. Less permanent assignments (public offices, clerical, chauffeurs, etc.) .. 212
3. Less details to special squads or divisions (traffic, vice, boat, etc.) 150

490

4. Average daily absentees of patrolmen assigned to patrol duty owing to:
5. Vacations and suspensions .... (33,580 days) 92
6. Sick and injured .... (10,111 ") 28
7. Temporary details ...., (19,207 ") 52

172

8. Available for patrol duty 318
Estimated population of the City of Buffalo 555,800
Appropriation fiscal year ending July 1, 1929 .... $3,172,968.82

TABLE III

Report of Police Surgeons

1. Number of times patrolmen reported sick or disabled .... 90£
   Number of times officers other than patrolmen reported sick or disabled .... 24(
2. Number of professional calls .... 3,69£
3. Number of days lost by sick leave .... { Patrolmen .... 10,11£
   { Other Officers .... 3,61£
4. Number of officers killed in line of duty .... £
5. Number of officers died (Active) .... 1£

Excerpt from the Charter of the City of Buffalo with reference to disability of members of the police department:

ARTICLE 12 SEC. 238. DISABILITY. The commissioner shall grant to each member of the department, when disabled by sickness, full pay for the time the disability exists, not, however to exceed a period of six months, and if a member of the department becomes disabled while in the performance of duty, full pay until he shall be able to resume his duty, for no longer period, however, than one year.

14

TABLE IV
NUMBER AND DISPOSITION OF MAJOR OFFENSES KNOWN TO THE POLICE

Shows Major Crimes brought to the attention of the police department from whatever source during the current year; whether by means of citizen's complaints, reports by police officers, or otherwise. If one is arrested who has committed ten burglaries, this would represent that number of burglaries cleared by arrest. In the "Unfounded" column are cases which investigation proved to be groundless. In the "Not Cleared" column are listed cases in which no arrests were made.

Nature of Offense	Offenses Known to the Police (current year)	Un-founded	Actual Cases	Cleared by Arrest	Not Cleared	Reported not cleared other years; Cleared
1. Murder*	14	—	14	5	8	4
2. Manslaughter:						
(a) Manslaughter—(except by Auto)	8	—	8	8	—	—
(b) Manslaughter—(Auto Death) ..	15	—	15	9	6	—
3. Rape	46	—	46	40	6	—
4. Robbery	242	4	238	109	129	18
5. Burglary—Breaking and Entering	856	4	852	479	373	23
6. Aggravated Assault	440	—	440	341	99	2
7. Larceny (except Autos)	1360	—	1360	920	440	—
8. Auto. Theft	2296	5	2291	379	1912	21
Grand Total	5277	13	5264	2290	2973	68

*One case cleared by suicide of the offender.

Homicides
FIRST PRECINCT

About 7:15 P.M. March 6, 1928, Salvatore Cuagliano, 38 years old, of 23 East Murray Street, Hamilton, Ontario, was shot and killed on Front Avenue between Carolina and Georgia Streets. Two men believed to be Italians jumped out of an automobile, shot Cuagliano, reentered the car which was driven rapidly away. No motive established and no persons arrested for this crime.

At 9 P.M. May 6, 1928, Stanley Lutz, age 29, of 68 Efner Street, was shot and killed in front of his home by two men. After the shooting the assailants were seen getting into a large dark colored sedan and left the scene hurriedly. No motive established and no persons arrested in connection with this crime.

About 10:15 P.M. May 7, 1928, Santo Falsone, 46 years old, of 1242 Niagara Street, was shot and killed in front of 168 Georgia Street while walking with his wife. Three men who took part in the killing of Falsone, left the scene in a large blue colored sedan. No motive established and no one arrested for this crime.

Sometime between 1:30 and 1:45 A.M. Sept. 19, 1928, Anthony Wietrzynski, 23 years old, of 149 Lombard Street, employed as a garbage wagon driver, was shot in the abdomen while in the basement of a soft drink place at 47 East Eagle Street, conducted by Eddie Przyble. Wietrzynski died a few hours later in the hospital. Later Lyman Miller, age 26, of 422 Jersey Street, was arrested and charged with Murder 1st Degree by Chief of Detectives John G. Reville, Detective Sergeants William J. Flynn, Bart O'Leary and John J. Fitzgerald. He was tried in the County Court and was acquitted.

About 6:10 P.M. December 14, 1928, Martin Ness, 39 years old, of 151 E. Eagle Street, became involved in an argument with Alex. Bach, 41 years old of 267 North Division Street, at North Division and Michigan Streets. Bach struck Ness on the jaw with his fist felling him; his head struck the curb and he became unconscious. He was removed to the Emergency Hospital and found to have a fractured skull. He died later. Bach was arrested by Captain William Coughlin, Detectives Phillips and Bingeman, Patrolman Thomas F. Caulfield and Francis V. Harrington and was indicted for Manslaughter. Case in pending.

SECOND PRECINCT

About 1:30 P.M. June 15, 1928, Joseph Weichman, age 46, a boarder in the home of Mrs. Katherine Wattles of 734 Perry Street was fatally shot in the head with a shotgun by Fred Wattles, 21 years old, son of Mrs. Wattles.

Weichman had been drinking heavily for some days and Mrs. Wattles had sworn out a warrant for him. He came to the Wattles home at this time, was denied admittance and threatened Mrs. Wattles. He attempted to enter the house by crawling through a window; while doing so he was shot. Fred Wattles was placed under arrest by Captain John Driscoll, Lieut. James Kennedy, Detectives Goetz, Murphy and Hofmeister, and Patrolman Leonard W.

Brooks. A charge of Manslaughter 1st Degree was placed against him and he was exonerated by the Grand Jury; a no bill being returned in this case.

About 9 P.M. July 28, 1928, Charles Salsbury, colored, rooming at 18 Myrtle Avenue, was fatally stabbed by James Johnson, colored man of the same address. The two men quarrelled over Ella Johnson, the common-law wife of James Johnson, the stabbing resulting. Salsbury was removed to the Emergency Hospital where he died.

The Johnsons came from Harrisburg, Pa., and for a time roomed at 28 Walnut Street. Johnson escaped and has not been apprehended for this crime.

About 11:30 A.M. August 12, 1928, Henry Suggs, colored, 37 years old of 27 Union Street, was shot and killed by Vivian Wilkeson, age 21, colored woman, in the house at 39 Pine Street, home of Mrs. Wilkeson.

At the above mentioned time Suggs came there looking for his wife and when told she was not there became angry and quarrelled with Mrs. Wilkeson; left the room threatening her. She procured a revolver from her bedroom and when Suggs returned with a bottle in each hand and advanced to strike her she fired two shots killing him instantly. She was arrested by Acting Captain James Kennedy, Detective Matthew G. Goetz and Patrolman William J. Leary on a charge of Murder 1st Degree. Mrs. Wilkeson was exonerated by the Grand Jury who returned a no bill in this case.

Shortly before 9 P.M. October 3, 1928, Alice Torpy, 26 years old and her mother, Mrs. Mary Rossiter, age 56, both of 812 Eagle Street, were cut with a razor by Vincent J. Torpy, husband of Alice Torpy. Torpy had been estranged from his wife for some time and called there to try and effect a reconciliation with his wife; Mrs. Rossiter interfered, picked up a hammer and struck Torpy on the head. The cutting resulted.

Mrs. Rossiter died in the Emergency Hospital from her wounds, her daughter recovered. Torpy was later arrested in an attic at 816 Eagle Street by Captain Driscoll, Lieutenant Hastings, Detectives Goetz, Hofmeister and Patrolmen Sparacino, Lynch, Harrington and Pilarski and a charge of Murder 1st Degree placed against him. An indictment for Manslaughter 1st Degree was returned against Torpy; the case is still pending.

At 1:30 P.M. October 31, 1928, Mrs. Mary Ladowski, age 70, proprietor of the Swan Hotel, 190 Swan Street, was shot and killed in the kitchen of the hotel by her son Stephen Ladowski, 30 years old of Forks, N. Y. Stephen came to see his mother while under the influence of liquor. She upraided him for his conduct, and when he asked her for financial assistance she refused him. He drew a revolver and shot her. Mrs. Ladowski died in the Emergency Hospital on November 5th.

Stephen was arrested some hours after the shooting at Forks, N. Y., by Captain Joseph Godfrey, Lieutenant William E. Downey, and Detectives Downey, Murphy, Fitzgibbons, Rogers, McNamara and Dewey of the Auto Squad. A charge of Murder 1st Degree was placed against him; an indictment charging Murder 2nd Degree was returned by the Grand Jury. Ladowski was allowed to plead guilty to a charge of Manslaughter 1st Degree and was sentenced to Auburn Prison for twenty years by Judge Rowe in the County Court.

THIRD PRECINCT

About 2:45 A.M. January 1, 1928, during a shooting affray in the Peacock Inn, 544 Washington Street, Michael George the proprietor of the place was killed and the following named patrons were injured: Wilbur Metz, 25 years old of 422 Pearl Street, shot in the right leg. Joseph Baggs, 26 years old of 103 Rodney Avenue, shot in the right arm. Eugene Grayson, 26 years old of 422 Pearl Street, shot in the left foot. Charlotte Gaiser, 20 years old of 495 Moselle Street, shot in the right temple.

A short time before the shooting three men entered the place, and started a disturbance and interfered with some of the patrons. The proprietor remonstrated with the men and during the argument revolvers were drawn, some wild shooting was done with the above mentioned results.

Arrests were made in this case but no positive identification of the men wanted was obtained and no one has been brought to trial.

At 7 o'clock A.M. June 10, 1928, Florence Topping, a rooming house keeper at 78 West Tupper Street, was found with her throat cut and died a short time later. Charles Zieman, 38 years old, a roomer, was accused of the crime, arrested and charged with Murder 1st Degree. He was tried and convicted of Manslaughter 1st Degree and sentenced to Auburn Prison for a term of 25 years. The crime was the result of a violent quarrel between the two.

About 5:45 A.M. July 12, 1928, John J. (Dot) Moriarity, 37 years old of 111 Crystal Avenue, was shot in the abdomen by Lloyd Danahy, age 28 of 385 McKinley Parkway, and died a short time later.

16

The shooting occurred in the soft drink place at 574 Washington Street conducted by John Danahy; the men quarrelled over a liquor transaction and the shooting resulted. Danahy left the scene of the shooting and evaded arrest for the time. Some hours later he was picked up at Port Colborne, Ontario, after an automobile accident and was turned over to our officers and returned to Buffalo. He was tried for Murder 1st Degree and was acquitted.

FOURTH PRECINCT

About 12:55 A.M. October 8, 1928, John Moore, alias Nappy Chin, age 46, of 437 Jefferson Avenue was shot in the right side and killed in front of 62 Mortimer Street. Moore and Pete Carson, both negroes, had been shaking dice in the house at 48 Mortimer Street, and the shooting is said to have been caused by a quarrel between the two over the game. Carson evaded arrest and has not been apprehended.

FIFTH PRECINCT

About 8:30 A.M. October 3, 1928, Arthur Post, age 49 of 67 Auburn Avenue was stabbed in the left groin with a pocket knife by Joseph Grifasi of 36 Ehlen Place, and died in the hospital on October 7th. Grifasi is the owner of the property at 67 Auburn Avenue and called there to collect the rent. The two men had an argument about the rent and during the quarrel Grifasi stabbed Post. Grifasi disappeared but was later arrested by Detective Soldano Frascella of the First Precinct and charged with Manslaughter 1st Degree. Case is pending.

SEVENTH PRECINCT

At 12:50 P.M. July 18, 1928, Michael Magker, 50 years old of 74 Abbott Road was arrested by Lieut. Henry J. Finsterbach, and Detectives Edwin J. McGuire and Roger Kane on a charge of Assault 1st Degree. Magker was accused of striking his wife Mary Magker, age 45 on the head with a hammer while she was lying in bed. She was removed to the Emergency Hospital and died on July 23rd from a fractured skull. Magker was then charged with Murder 1st Degree and on December 10th pleaded Guilty to a charge of Murder 2nd Degree and was sentenced to Auburn Prison for a term of 20 years to Life.

At 1:25 A.M. December 22, 1928, Patrolman Harold Haltam was shot four times in the back and legs while attempting to arrest three men whom he surprised burglarizing the packing house of Armour & Co., 228 Perry Street. A window had been jimmied by the burglars and one of them was inside the building while two stood outside when surprised by the officer. After shooting the officer the three men made their escape abandoning an automobile on a nearby street. Haltam was removed to the Emergency Hospital where he died at 10 P.M. the same day.

At 2:50 A.M. about one hour later Patrolmen Peter Dominack and Robert Kuhn arrested two men whom they found near the Keystone Warehouse at Hamburg and Seneca Streets and sent them to No. 2 Police Station. They proved to be Arthur W. Brown, age 36 of 43 Florida Street and John Schlager, 32 years old of 51 Kilhoffer Street; both men have bad criminal records. Further investigation connected them with the killing of Patrolman Haltam and they were held on a charge of Murder 1st Degree. At 7:30 A.M. December 24th, Frank Kowalski, aged 25 was arrested in his home at 239 Peckham Street, by Chief of Detectives Reville, Detective Sergeants Burns, Mahaney, John J. Fitzgerald, Walter Holz and Patrolman Daniel Goodman. He was found to be suffering from bullet wounds believed to have been inflicted by one of his pals when firing at the officer. A charge of Murder 1st Degree was also placed against him.

The three men have since been tried and convicted of the crime charged and sentenced to die in the electric chair.

TENTH PRECINCT

About 1 A.M. May 17, 1928, Russell Borzelleri, age 33 of 288 Front Avenue was shot four times and killed as he was coming down the rear stairway of his home. Rose Borzelleri, his wife, age 32 was arrested by Detective Sergeants Kenny, Smaldino and Gustaferro, accused of the crime and a charge of Murder 1st Degree placed against her. She was tried and convicted of Manslaughter 1st Degree and was sentenced to Auburn Prison for a term of 6 to 10 years.

About 3:30 A.M. July 27, 1928, during a quarrel at Allen and Wadsworth Streets, John Murphy, 27 years old of 78 Days Park struck Fred Gamlin, age 52 of 109 Mariner Street with his fist, felling him. His head struck the sidewalk and he become unconscious. He was removed to the hospital and died a few hours later from a fractured skull. Murphy was held on a charge of Manslaughter 1st Degree and was convicted of Assault 3rd Degree and was sentenced to one year in the Erie County Penitentiary.

Arresting officers Captain Fred G. Eckner, Lieut. Wm. F. Grossman, Detective Wm. E. Jordan and Patrolman George Tidd.

About 1:40 P.M. August 4, 1928, Milton A. Harris, age 25 of 1464 Michigan Avenue, shot and killed Louise Friday, 20 years old of 237 Connecticut Street, a telephone operator for the New York Telephone Company, in the Tupper Exchange. Harris followed the girl in an automobile to the corner of North and Arlington Place where the shooting took place. The motive for the crime appears to have been jealousy, and due to the girl refusing further attentions from him; the two had been keeping company and quarrelled. After shooting the girl Harris turned the gun on himself, the bullet causing a slight flesh wound in the head. He was tried for Murder 1st Degree, convicted and sentenced to death in the electric chair.

Arresting officers, George T. Melody and Alfred M. Reidel.

About 9:30 A.M. October 31, 1928, Frank Merolla, age 43 of 496 Seventh Street, engaged in the painting and decorating business, went to his garage for his truck. According to his wife he was gone from the house about five minutes when there was an explosion. Investigation showed that Merolla evidently stepped on the starter of the truck, which set off a bomb, connected with the starter. The explosion wrecked the garage completely, both of Merolla's legs were blown off and he was severely burned about the body, death resulting a short time later in the Columbus Hospital. No motive was definitely established for the crime and no one brought to trial up to this time.

ELEVENTH PRECINCT

About 11:10 A.M. April 25, 1928, Sherbourne Wilder, age 32, married, of 21 Tacoma Avenue, an electrician employed by the Lovejoy Electric Company, 1144 Lovejoy Street, was shot in the neck by an unknown man who attempted to rob the cashier of the store. Wilder died a few minutes later. His assailant has not been apprehended.

About 11:30 A.M. May 14, 1928, Elizabeth Piotrowska, age 33, married, of 55 Brownell Street, cut the throat of her year-old son as he lay in his crib, causing his death. She then attempted suicide by cutting her own throat and wrists with the same razor. She was committed to the City Hospital for treatment and observation as to her sanity, and later was declared insane by the examining physicians and committed to the State Hospital for the insane.

FIFTEENTH PRECINCT

At 9 P.M. August 20, 1928, Arthur W. Rodgers, 56 years old of No. 140 Macamley Street, went to the assistance of a young woman who was attempting to get out of an automobile which was parked across the street from his home. During the fight which ensued with Gerald Dempsey, 20 years old of 356 Cumberland Avenue, the driver of the car, Rodgers was struck in the face by Dempsey and fell to the street and became unconscious. He was removed to the Mercy Hospital where he died on September 2nd from a fracture of the skull.

Dempsey evaded arrest at the time but was later apprehended and held. He was indicted for Manslaughter 1st Degree, tried and acquitted.

SIXTEENTH PRECINCT

At 6:30 P.M. December 8, 1928, George Faxlanger, age 51 of 34 Demond Place shot and killed his wife Mary Faxlanger, age 50 of 20 Martha Street, in front of 3006 Bailey Avenue with a Winchester rifle.

The Faxlangers had been separated about six months. Faxlanger waylaid his wife as she was returning from a store and fired one shot which struck her in the head; a stray shot struck Albert Novy, age 15 of 163 Hastings Street, who was passing at the time, in the right arm. Faxlanger then turned the gun on himself, firing a shot into the top of his head which resulted fatally. He carried the rifle in two lengths of stove pipe to conceal it from view as he approached his wife. Both were dead when the City Hospital ambulance arrived.

Investigating Officers, Captain Edward N. Rast, Lieut. Eugene H. Radtke, Detective Charles T. Vickers and Patrolman George C. Craine.

TABLE IV-A
Distribution of Certain Offenses; by Month.

Nature of Offense	Jan.	Feb.	Mar.	Apr.	May	June	July	Aug.	Sept.	Oct.	Nov.	Dec.
1. Robbery	18	15	12	17	14	10	18	20	22	26	24	42
2. Burglary—Breaking and Entering	70	97	73	75	80	63	49	52	52	73	84	84
3. Aggravated Assault	36	33	40	47	39	37	32	39	27	47	29	34
4. Larceny—(except Auto Theft)	86	128	101	134	145	136	111	91	97	101	114	116
5. Auto Theft	233	193	197	216	181	176	175	139	138	172	224	247
6. Disorderly Conduct and Vagrancy	472	461	450	450	446	303	432	390	394	392	570	290
7. Drunkenness	564	509	634	613	869	779	793	725	789	841	776	673
Total	1479	1436	1507	1552	1774	1504	1610	1456	1519	1652	1821	1486

TABLE IV-B
Distribution of Certain Offenses; By Hour of Day

Nature of Offense	12 M'D. to 2 A.M.	2 A.M. to 4 A.M.	4 A.M. to 6 A.M.	6 A.M. to 8 A.M.	8 A.M. to 10A.M.	10 A.M. to 12 M.	12 M. to 2 P.M.	2 P.M. to 4 P.M.	4 P.M. to 6 P.M.	6 P.M. to 8 P.M.	8 P.M. to 10 P.M.	10 P.M. to 12 M'D.	Unknown
1. Robbery	33	29	23	11	5	7	8	12	11	23	36	40	......
2. Burglary	84	146	127	68	11	20	19	39	18	25	65	78	152
3. Assault	64	35	31	10	33	30	27	38	23	42	55	52	......
4. Larceny—Theft (except Auto Theft)	91	78	60	35	82	120	119	171	152	126	159	107	60
5. Auto Theft	275	80	34	65	102	69	61	101	150	390	597	319	48
6. Disorderly Conduct and Vagrancy	963	643	220	167	187	314	269	384	371	335	505	692	......
7. Drunkenness	1460	877	463	191	320	498	512	759	646	685	935	1219	......
Total	2970	1888	958	547	740	1058	1015	1504	1371	1626	2352	2507	260

TABLE IV-C

	Number of Major Offenses Known to the Police Per 100,000 Inhabitants 1928	Per Cent. of Major Offenses Cleared by Arrest 1928
1. Murder	2.5	36
2. Manslaughter: (a) Manslaughter (except by Auto.)	1.4	100
(b) Manslaughter (Auto Deaths)	2.7	60
3. Rape	8.3	87
4. Robbery	43.2	46
5. Burglary, Breaking and Entering	154.9	56
6. Aggravated Assault	80	78
7. Larceny (except Auto. Theft)	247.2	68
8. Auto. Theft	416.5	17
Grand Total	956.7	44

TABLE V

Apprehensions and Conviction for Major and Miscellaneous Offenses

		Apprehensions Resulting in Prosecution			CONVICTIONS	
Nature of Offense		Arrested	Summoned	Total	Of Offense Charged	Of Lesser Offense
MAJOR OFFENSES:						
1.	Murder	7		7	5	0
2.	Manslaughter:					
	(a) Manslaughter (except by Auto.)	8		8	3	1
	(b) Manslaughter—Auto. Death	9		9	0	0
3.	Rape	60		60	25	6
4.	Robbery	192		192	63	45
5.	Burglary—Breaking and Entering	425		425	202	110
6.	Aggravated Assault	442		442	165	111
7.	Larceny (except Auto. Theft)	1,248		1,248	653	107
8.	Auto. Theft	303		303	144	119
	Total Major Offenses	2,694		2,694	1,260	499
	MISCELLANEOUS OFENSES:					
9.	Other Assaults	1,238		1,238	571	66
10.	Forgery	47		47	24	6
11.	Carrying Weapons	175		175	130	1
12.	Sex Offenses, except Rape	305		305	132	0
13.	Offenses against Family and Children	789		789	579	2
14.	Violating Drug Laws*	20		20	2	0
15.	Violating Liquor Laws*	284		284	14	0
16.	Driving while Intoxicated	314		314	131	16
17.	Drunkenness	8,565		8,565	7,976	0
18.	Disorderly Conduct and Vagrancy	5,050		5,050	3,920	0
19.	Gambling	993		993	768	0
20.	Viol. Traffic and Motor Vehicle Laws	262	18,051	18,313	15,496	70
21.	All other	2,897		2,897	2,100	8
	Total Misc. Offenses	20,939	18,051	38,990	31,843	169

*Violation of Drug and Liquor Cases turned over to Federal Authorities.

TABLE V-A

Summary of Major Offenses known to police apprehensions and dispositions—1928

Table V-A is a summary of Tables IV and V and indicates what is actually accomplished in the way of clea
ing cases and securing convictions of persons apprehended.

Nature of Offense			
1.	Murder	36	71
2.	Manslaughter:		
	(a) Manslaughter (except by Auto.)	100	38
	(b) Manslaughter (Auto. Deaths)	60	—
3.	Rape	87	42
4.	Robbery	46	33
5.	Burglary—Breaking and Entering	56	48
6.	Aggravated Assault	78	37
7.	Larceny (except Auto. Theft)	68	52
8.	Auto. Theft*	17	48

*441 persons were arrested for auto. theft, 138 of this number were charged with the more serious offen
of robbery or burglary.

TABLE V-B

Apprehension for Violation of Traffic and Motor Vehicle Laws.

Nature of Violation	Apprehensions Resulting in Prosecution		
	Number Arrested	Summoned	Total
1. Speeding	43	1,473	1,516
2. Reckless Driving	76	699	775
3. Illegal Parking	8	2,478	2,486
4. Improper or Defective Lights or Brakes	3	610	613
5. Non-observance of signal light or Traffic Sign	34	10,999	11,033
6. Improper Registration or License	17	332	349
7. Other	81	1,460	1,541
.Total	262	18,051	18,313

TABLE VI

Apprehensions for certain offenses according to Nativity,
Color and Citizenship

Nature of Offenses	Native White	Foreign Born White	Negro	Indian Chinese Japanese and Other	Mexican	Citizen	Alien
Major Offenses:							
1. Murder	6	1				6	1
2. Manslaughter:							
Manslaughter, (except by Auto.)	5	2	1			7	1
Manslaughter, (Auto. Death)	8	1				9	
3. Rape	43	8	8	1		57	3
4. Robbery	137	23	30	1	1	182	10
5. Burglary—Breaking and							
Entering	353	37	33	1	1	410	15
6. Aggravated Assault	192	91	154	4	1	401	41
7. Larceny (except Auto. Theft)	858	296	86	8		1,171	77
8. Auto. Theft	252	42	7	2		293	10
Miscellaneous Offenses:							
9. Other Assaults	873	235	126	1	3	1,148	90
10. Forgery	41	6				46	1
11. Carrying Weapons	88	49	37	1		164	11
12. Sex Offenses, except Rape	208	31	66			286	19
13. Offenses against Family &							
Children	635	142	12			743	46
14. Violating Drug Laws	15	2	3			19	1
15. Violating Liquor Laws	187	88	9			259	25
16. Drunkenness	6,080	1,624	783	18	60	7,982	583
17. Disorderly Conduct							
and Vagrancy	3,056	838	1,087	39	30	4,515	535
18. Gambling	789	51	126	12	15	970	23

TABLE VII

Apprehensions for Certain Offenses; by Age and Sex

Major Offenses	Under 16 Juveniles M	F	16 M	F	17 M	F	18-19 M	F	20-24 M	F	25-29 M	F	30-34 M	F	35-39 M	F	40-44 M	F	Over 44 M	F	Total M	F
1. Murder	—	—	—	—	—	—	—	—	1	—	2	—	1	1	1	—	—	—	1	—	6	1
2. Manslaughter	—	—	—	—	—	—	1	—	5	—	3	—	2	1	2	—	1	—	2	—	16	1
3. Rape	3	—	2	—	3	—	16	—	20	—	11	—	2	—	—	—	1	—	2	—	60	—
4. Robbery	2	—	11	—	12	—	23	—	64	1	33	1	27	2	6	—	8	—	2	—	188	4
5. Burglary, Breaking and Entering	133	—	22	—	27	—	51	—	68	—	44	—	35	—	24	—	7	—	12	—	423	2
6. Aggravated Assault	3	—	3	—	1	—	16	—	67	19	94	18	65	6	48	8	37	5	47	5	381	61
7. Larceny (except Auto Theft)	208	7	49	7	38	8	82	10	129	30	137	17	136	36	107	32	91	22	87	15	1,064	184
8. Auto Theft	39	4	26	—	29	—	57	—	74	1	37	—	19	1	12	—	4	—	—	—	297	6
Miscellaneous Offenses																						
9. Other Assaults	11	—	10	2	16	—	38	7	185	24	201	20	216	25	164	24	112	12	156	15	1,109	129
10. Forgery	—	—	—	—	1	—	1	1	4	—	7	1	9	1	8	—	3	1	9	1	42	5
11. Carrying Weapons	3	—	2	1	1	—	12	—	27	2	34	2	34	1	25	2	17	—	12	—	167	8
12. Sex Offenses except Rape	—	—	—	—	3	3	4	—	9	49	19	69	15	44	6	32	11	19	9	13	76	229
13. Viol. Drug Laws	—	—	—	—	—	—	—	—	1	—	5	2	4	—	1	—	5	—	2	—	18	2
14. Viol. Liquor Laws	—	—	1	—	1	—	5	—	40	—	39	5	50	—	34	8	46	—	45	10	261	23
15. Drunkenness	1	—	11	—	15	—	109	1	619	36	1,043	69	1,147	69	1,202	99	1,671	97	2,224	152	8,042	523
16. Disorderly Conduct and Vagrancy	17	3	47	3	60	7	176	37	494	129	703	122	677	84	698	102	706	50	894	41	4,472	578
17. Gambling	2	—	14	—	7	—	108	—	179	1	182	1	139	1	125	—	109	—	125	—	990	3

TABLE VIII
AUTO THEFTS and RECOVERIES

		1928	1927	1926	1925	1924
1.	Automobiles reported stolen in the city	2,291	2,444	2,567	1,904	2,451
2.	Recovered by Auto. Squad	535	619	583	316	504
3.	Recovered by Other Officers	1,379	1,436	1,578	1,224	1,535
4.	Recovered by authorities of other Jurisdictions	308	324	242	241	283
5.	Total Recovered (stolen in the City)	2,222	2,379	2,403	1,781	2,322
6.	Per Cent. of stolen autos. recovered	95	94.7	92.8	91.9	93.7
7.	Automobiles recovered for other Jurisdictions	133	134	86	119	109
8.	Automobiles still missing after 24 hours	654	745	737	682	
9.	Automobiles recovered stolen other years	45	63	39	31	25
10.	Personnel of Automobile Squad	1 Lieutenant and 21 detectives				
11.	Personnel of Automobile Record Bureau	1 Desk Lieutenant and 7 patrolmen				
12.	Automobile license registration (pleasure vehicles)	149,985	140,000	129,540	125,500	101,000

TABLE IX
Value of Property reported lost or stolen and recovered
by Police Department
(AUTOMOBILES NOT INCLUDED)

Property reported lost or stolen	$242,004.79
1. Recovered by pawn shop squad	13,073.00
2. Recovered by other police units	68,472.92
Total property recovered	81,545.92
Property recovered for other jurisdictions	6,557.25

TABLE X
Miscellaneous Services Rendered by Police Department

	Nature of Services	1928		Nature of Services	1928
1.	Doors found and reported open	2,584	8.	Apprehensions for other jurisdictions	391
2.	Persons reported to the police as missing	925	9.	Lunacy cases handled	132
3.	Missing persons found (including		10.	Suicide cases investigated	59
	children)	888	11.	Sudden deaths investigated	130
4.	Fires discovered	683	12.	Wagon service:	
5.	Lamp outages reported	28,142		a. Number of runs for prisoners	7,391
6.	Non-criminal complaints investigated	38,827		b. Number of runs for sick and injured	547
7.	Non-vehicular accidents	249		c. Other	10,468

TABLE X-A
Report of the Bureau of Identification

Identification of criminals arrested locally	125	Received from other authorities and filed	1,688
Identification of criminals arrested elsewhere	103	Number on file December 31, 1928	24,988
Scenes of crimes photographed	20		
Latent prints obtained and photographed	21	PHOTOGRAPHS SENT TO	
		Bureau of Investigation, U. S. Department	
PHOTOGRAPH FILE		of Justice	1,872
Number on file December 31, 1927	20,015	State Bureau of Identification	1,872
Made and filed during the year	2,052	Other cities and states	400
Received from other authorities and filed	1,500		
Number on file December 31, 1928	23,567	FINGERPRINTS SENT TO	
		Bureau of Investigation, U. S. Department	
FINGERPRINT FILE		of Justice	2,013
Number on file December 31, 1927	21,000	State Bureau of Identification	2,013
Taken and filed during the year	2,300	Other cities and states	400

TABLE XI

Distribution of Plant and Equipment

Nature of Information	Totals of all Precincts	PRECINCTS 1	2	3	4	5	6	7	8	9	10
and Valuation of Building (not including land)		$40,000	$42,340	$7,265	$28,600	$39,600	$21,550	$23,720	$57,200	$16,500	$23,930
Year		1884	1915	1881	1891	1895	1883	1879	1915	1885	1891
Area in square miles	42	1.65	0.72	0.87	0.78	2.19	2.72	3.90	1.49	3.07	1.38
Real miles of streets	648.30	16.81	21.47	26.43	20.91	39.10	54.79	24.13	38.85	45.01	24.31
Number of ambulances	1										
Number of motor patrols	7							1	1	1	
Number of automobiles	58	2	1	2	1	2	2	1	2	1	2
Number of motorcycles	39					1	1	1	1	1	1
Number of patrol boxes and booths	98	12		12						12	
Number of patrol with call boxes	471	58	35	53	40	70	85	29	39	1	62
Number of phone switchboards	11	1	1	1	1	1	1	1	1	1	1
Number of interconnecting telephones	664	58	35	53	40	70	85	29	39	12	62
Number of storage battery and power plants	10	1	1	1	1	1	1	1	1	1	1
Number of storage batteries	870	24	24	24	24	24	24	24	24		24
Number of pawn shop boxes	26	22		3	1						
Number of bank line boxes	12	7		5	1						
Number of fire telegraph line sections	25	1	1	1	1	1	1	1	1	1	1
Number of Fire Alarm boxes	22	1	1	1	1	1	1	2	1	1	1
Number of Automatic Traffic Signals	249	12	6	42	19	19	33	2	13	7	16
Number of Illuminated Direction & Designation Signs	35	12		10			1	5			1
Number of signals interconnected	45	7		29			9				
Number of Traffic signals interconnected "Synchronized System"	24	1									
Number of Illuminated Traffic Stop by Signs	9	1		2	2	3	3	3	4	2	3
Number of Illuminated Standards on Safety Islands	23	4		17					2		
Number of miles of underground cable 16 to 125 pair	68.94	6.72	5.68	9.13	6.32	12.87	16.66	1.00	4.26		6.30

Headquarters and No. 1 are in the same building.

TABLE XI (Continued)

Distribution of Plant and Equipment

Nature of Information	Totals of all Precincts	11	12	13	14	15	16	17	Sub 17	Headquarters	Garage Ferry St.	Garage Henry St.
Assessed Valuation of Building (not including land)		$24,000	$52,800	$30,830	$17,875	$14,070	$32,500	$12,500	—	*Same as $1	$115,800	$18,160
Year built	42	1885	1911	1894	1885	1902	1925	1927	1904		1921	
Area in square miles	648.30	3.10	4.06	3.05	3.15	3.66	3.23	2.41	0.57			
Lineal miles of ... sets	1	36.94	55.26	41.74	51.29	40.89	65.11	39.76	5.50			
... of ... this com	7											
... of motor patrols	58	1	2	1	2	2	2	1	1	28	1	
... of automobiles	89	1	1	2	1	1	1	1	2	24	1	
Number of motorcycles	98	10	23	1	10	11	10	9				
... of patrol boxes and booths	471			13								
... of patrol with light boxes	11		1	13		1	1	1	1	1	1	
... of telephone switchboards	664	10	23	13	10	11	10	9		85	10	
N ... of interconnecting telephones	10									1		
... of storage battery and power plants	870									654		
... of storage batteries	26											
... of ... shop boxes	12	1	1	1	1	1	1	1	1	8		
... of bank line boxes	25	1	1	1	1	1	1	1	4	5		
Number of Morse telegraph line connections	22	8	29	9	16	7	2	8				
... of Fire Alarm Conn this	249					2						
Number of Automatic Traffic Signals	35											
... of Illuminated ... Ekon & Designation Signs	45		2	2			2	1				
... of Traffic ... interconnected	24											
... of Traffic signals "Cronoplan System" erected	9											
Number of Illuminated Traffic Stop Highway Signs	23											
... Standards on Safety Islands												
... of miles of underground lead cable 15 to 125 pair	68.94											

25

TABLE XII

"Accident summary, year 1928, City of Buffalo"

TYPE OF ACCIDENT AND AGE GROUP

(TYPE OF ACCIDENT)	(NUMBER OF PERSONS KILLED)					(NUMBER OF PERSONS INJURED)				
	All Ages	0—4	5—14	15—54	55 & Over	All Ages	0—4	5—14	15—54	55 & Over
GRAND TOTAL—	143	9	24	44	66	3,104	157	602	1,999	346
MOTOR VEHICLE TOTAL—	122	9	23	39	51	3,045	155	598	1,954	338
Motor Vehicle with pedestrian	100	9	22	20	49	1,558	126	496	714	222
Motor Vehicle with motor vehicle	10		1	7	2	1,183	27	82	991	83
Motor Vehicle with railroad train	2			2		5			4	1
Motor Vehicle with electric car	3			3		141	1	5	118	18
Motor Vehicle with bicycle						43		13	23	6
Motor Vehicle with horse drawn vehicle						24		1	22	1
Motor Vehicle with animal						1			1	
Motor Vehicle with fixed object	4			4		75	1	1	69	4
Non-Collision operating accident	3			3		15			12	3
NOT MOTOR VEHICLE TOTAL—	21		1	5	15	59	2	4	45	8
Railroad—not with motor vehicle	3			1	2					
Electric Car—not with motor vehicle	18		1	4	13	50	2	4	40	8
Other Vehicle—not with motor vehicle						9			5	

CIRCUMSTANCES ATTENDING OCCURRENCE OF MOTOR VEHICLE ACCIDENTS

(LOCATION)	(NUMBER OF ACCIDENTS)			(TYPE OF VEHICLE)	(NUMBER OF VEHICLES)		
	Total	Fatal	Non-Fatal		Total	Fatal	Non-Fatal
Railroad crossing	7	1	6	Private passenger car	2,938	108	2,830
On bridge	17	1	16	Truck or commercial	328	18	310
At intersection	1,662	54	1,608	Taxicab	58	3	55
Not at intersection	899	66	833	Bus	13	2	11
				Motorcycle	27	1	26

	Total	Fatal	Non-Fatal
Number of Accidents Reported		122	2,463
Total	2,585		

(RESIDENCE OF DRIVER)

(Number of Drivers)

	Total	Fatal	Non-Fatal
Unknown	9	4	5
Out of State	47	1	46
Out of City	380	15	365
Resident of city	2,886	97	2,789

(AGE OF DRIVER)

Unknown	11	6	5
Under 16 years	2		2
16 years	2		2
17 years	5		5
18 to 24 years	911	35	876
25 to 54 years	2,134	70	2,064
55 years and over	134	6	128

(SEX OF DRIVER)

Unknown	2	2	
Male	3,137	123	3,014
Female	199	8	191

(ACTION OF DRIVERS)

Turning right	75	3	72
Turning left	274	9	265
Going straight through	2,746	105	2,641
Slowing down or stopping	143	2	141
Backing	37	1	36
Parked or standing still	81	2	79
Skidding	48	4	44

(ACTION OF DRIVER)
Violations

Exceeding the speed limit	24	8	16
On wrong side of road	19	5	14
Did not have right of way	11	9	2
Cutting in	4		4
Passing standing street car	9	1	8
Passing on wrong side	10	1	9
Failed to signal	7		7
Improper turning	3		3
Failed to stop—through highway or street	1		1
Disregarded officer or signal	32	2	30
Drove off roadway	3	3	

(CONDITION OF DRIVER)

Was intoxicated	14		14
Was asleep	1		1
Extreme fatigue	8		8

(CONDITION OF VEHICLE)

Defective brakes	3	1	2
Defect in steering mechanism	5	1	4
Other defects	1	1	

(SEX OF PEDESTRIAN)

Male	1,069	76	993
Female	589	24	565

(THE PEDESTRIAN)

(Number of Pedestrians)

	Total	Fatal	Non-Fatal
Crossing at intersection with signal	30	2	28
Crossing at intersection against signal	77	7	70
Crossing at intersection no signal	624	16	608
Crossing at intersection diagonally	17	6	11
Crossing between intersections	482	49	433
Playing in street	84	5	79
Riding or hitching on vehicle	23	1	22
Waiting for or getting on or off street car at safety zone	13	1	12
Waiting for or getting on or off street car no safety zone	64	2	62
Getting on or off other vehicles	5	1	4
At work in roadway	25		25
Not in roadway	20	4	16
Other actions	114	2	112

(CONDITION OF PEDESTRIAN)

Pedestrian was intoxicated	18	1	17
Was confused by traffic	52	6	46
View obstructed	6		6

(ROAD SURFACE CONDITION)

Dry surface	276	76	200
Wet surface	15	7	8
Snowy surface	2	2	
Icy surface	45	1	44

(WEATHER CONDITION)

Clear	1,647	83	1,564
Cloudy	541	28	513
Fog	5		5
Rain	314	9	305
Snow	79	2	77

(LIGHT CONDITION)

Daylight	1,392	58	1,334
Dusk	20	1	19
Darkness, good artificial light	1,165	63	1,102
Darkness, poor artificial light	2		2
Darkness, no artificial light	6		6

PISTOL RANGE

A pleasing report for the year 1928 was made by the pistol range instructors. A marked improvement was noticed in the markmanship of officers whose progress was slow the year previous. A good percentage of the men have qualified as experts or sharpshooters, which is not only an asset to the department, but gratifying to the Commissioner and the men in charge of the work.

Members of the department are required to shoot at the department range at least once a month. The scores made are recorded and any needed instructions given to help the officer improve his markmanship. Great interest has been shown in this activity since the range was placed in service, members spent their own time in practicing on the station house ranges preparing for the monthly shoot. Those who are now proficient in the art of revolver shooting and the care of firearms will benefit when taking promotional examinations as credit marks will be given for this subject.

Our revolver team was very successful in competition winning nine out of eleven matches with teams from other departments and organizations.

During the year three patrolmen were shot by criminals, one fatally, while five persons were shot by officers attempting to escape arrest, one was fatal.

STOLEN PROPERTY
Miscellaneous

	Value of Property Reported Lost	Value of Property Found	Value of Property Reported Stolen	Value of Property Recovered	Value of Property Recovered for Other Authorities
Headquarters			$24,795.35	$29,134.54	$4,704.00
Precinct No. 1	$ 163.70	$ 65.00	9,468.01	2,440.00	500.00
Precinct No. 2	89.50	89.50	9,865.50	4,251.25	385.00
Precinct No. 3	1,397.55	25.00	41,511.41	6,550.50	
Precinct No. 4	101.00	50.00	10,417.90	2,335.80	
Precinct No. 5			2,728.00	729.50	100.00
Precinct No. 6			10,676.95	1,542.20	
Precinct No. 7	215.88	215.88	8,679.09	2,083.20	75.00
Precinct No. 8	359.00	25.00	19,955.12	2,889.02	
Precinct No. 9	173.90	16.90	6,075.90	1,253.25	
Precinct No. 10	498.50	393.00	10,128.46	2,303.45	
Precinct No. 11			2,894.97	759.40	125.00
Precinct No. 12	878.00	566.00	37,421.65	2,710.97	395.00
Precinct No. 13	298.00	200.00	10,563.93	7,586.30	
Precinct No. 14	184.50	89.50	8,673.61	4,648.47	273.25
Precinct No. 15	142.60	60.00	1,011.47	731.87	
Precinct No. 16	125.00	125.00	11,068.08	6,596.60	
Precinct No. 17	297.50	155.00	10,897.76	923.82	
Precinct Sub. 17			247.00		
Totals	$4,924.63	$2,075.78	$237,080.16	$79,470.14	$6,557.25

MARITAL CONDITIONS

Precincts	Married	Single	Total
Headquarters	·3,644	4,263	7,907
No. 1	3,000	3,450	6,450
No. 2	1,097	1,283	2,380
No. 3	2,200	2,449	4,649
No. 4	1,770	1,941	3,711
No. 5	361	416	777
No. 6	367	443	810
No. 7	581	647	1,228
No. 8	1,126	1,261	2,387
No. 9	518	614	1,132
No. 10	878	980	1,858
No. 11	742	806	1,548
No. 12	811	911	1,722
No. 13	688	786	1,474
No. 14	428	313	741
No. 15	454	542	996
No. 16	494	588	1,082
No. 17	331	436	767
Sub. 17	55	10	65
Total	19,545	22,139	41,684

ARRESTS BY PRECINCTS

Precincts	Male	Female	Total
Headquarters	7,411	496	7,907
No. 1	6,029	421	6,450
No. 2	1,894	486	2,380
No. 3	4,009	640	4,649
No. 4	3,304	407	3,711
No. 5	722	55	777
No. 6	755	55	810
No. 7	1,173	55	1,228
No. 8	2,179	208	2,387
No. 9	1,074	58	1,132
No. 10	1,724	134	1,858
No. 11	1,441	107	1,548
No. 12	1,642	80	1,722
No. 13	1,356	118	1,474
No. 14	702	39	741
No. 15	945	51	996
No. 16	1,051	31	1,082
No. 17	719	48	767
Sub. 17	51	14	65
Total	38,181	3,503	41,684

SQUAD DETAILS

	H.D.	1	2	3	4	5	6	7	8	9	10	11	12	13	14	15	16	17	Sub 17	Totals
Bicycle Squad	1			1	1	1	1	1	1	1	2	1	1	1	1	1	1	1	2	20
Headquarters Motorcycle Squad	1	1	1	1	1	1	1	1	1	1	2	1	1	1	1	1	1	–	2	21
Precinct Motorcycle Squad						1	1	1	1	1	1	1	1	1	1	1	1	1		14
Mounted Squad*	27																			27
Patrol Boat	9				2															9
Traffic Squad*	26			31			2													59

Total 150

*Squads are on duty the year around.

Members of the H.D. Motorcycle Squad during the Winter season are engaged in various duties in connection with traffic.

Members of the Patrol Boat, precinct bicycle and motorcycle squads become foot patrolmen during the Winter season in their respective precincts.

TEMPORARY DETAIL SCHEDULE

	1	2	3	4	5	6	7	8	9	10	11	12	13	14	15	16	17	Sub 17	Total Hours
Athletics, Misc.	62		18		25	77	7			186	12	65	616	51	1	61	12		474
Baseball		110	121	94	186	1,064			619	186	9			312	63	301	325		3,905
Basketball			47	157	83	50				170	4	127	41	165		67	23		560
Boxing		320	94	616	169		16	681	62	191	8	1,183	52	44	36	210	124	36	2,560
Band Concerts	405	20	37	8	50		57		244	62	109	860	19	656	428	13	25		2,696
Banks	72	100	758	212	621		40		128	437	172		19	19		432	692		7,709
Carnivals			41	170	38				104		4	166		7	20	4			677
Circus		20	13	27									8	5			42		582
Conventions		40	28	20	65					6			62				42		252
Concerts			89							131									57
Cashiers																			
Dances	160	500	362	26	57	291	106	792	181	237	82	247	234	161	35	276	47		3,763
Fires	18	250	20	46	187	43	116	141	56	104	258	86	9	119	14	76	47		1,683
Fireworks	5	80	80	74	144				70	12	19		16	28	4	11	19		296
Football	118	55	60	29	42	388	78	63	138	90	75	204	204	10		66	66		1,457
Funerals		96	120	100	5	83		46	54	48	47	12	24	24	27	55	9		957
Federal raids																			
Hospitals	28	1,300	15	123			40		567		184	1,240	67	232	1,426	682			5,003
Ice Skating	16	30		16										6	23	17	33		993
Lawn Fetes				14															14
Meetings	1,900	400	1,512	41	34	36	41		299	83	8	120	1,414	308	2	16	32		1,840
Paymasters			1,145	32		52	233	1,101			916			147	45	29	20		8,035
Parades											404			13		150			753
Regattas																			28
Schools	1,473	2,400	1,884	1,592	1,742	3,000	1,262	3,357	1,716	1,566	1,699	382	2,422	3,908	2,740	3,217	2,400		36,760
Street Dances			15	36	6														41
Strikes	2						1,735	63	120	18	380	1,151	264	96	80	77	1,466		3,859
Theatres			632	18	84					413			3	30	3	28	1,329		2,330
Traffic			405	103					2,129			109	1,873	220	2,684				9,293
Vice						36				15				320					320
Weddings			139		6		36					420		8		7			205
Wrestling																			
Miscellaneous	2,777	1,100		919	1,595	5,468	9,648	2,657	6,496	1,659	5,575		1,391	508	153	1,658	692	418	58,477
Total Hours	7,025	6,950	28,029	4,525	5,121	10,601	13,378	8,800	12,883	5,827	9,972	5,308	9,993	7,585	7,781	7,478	7,451	454	153,661

153,661 hours lost in one year.
489 hours lost in one day.
52 men taken from patrol force each day.

1 year—365 days.
1 tour— 8 hours.

PERMANENT DETAILS OF PATROLMEN

Detail	H.D.	1	2	3	4	5	6	7	8	9	10	11	12	13	14	15	16	17	Sub 17	Total
Airport	2																			2
Art Gallery																			1	1
Auto. Patrols	6	7			6		3		6	6										34
Auto. Record Bureau	5											1	1							7
Auto. Squad	6							1												7
Bertillion Department	6			1									1							8
Chauffeurs														6						6
Childrens Court											1									1
City Court	3																			5
City Treasurer	1																			1
Corporation Counsel	2																			2
Dept. Commissioner (nights)	1											1	1							3
Detective Bureau	2																			2
Dry Squad	1					1														2
Garage, E. Ferry Street							1													2
Garage, Broadway																				1
Garage, Henry Street																				2
Health Department	1																			1
Lost and Stolen Prop. Bureau	2			4				5	3											15
Markets																				2
Mounted Barn	2																			2
Paymasters (city) office																				1
Parks*																				3
Peace Bridge	2																			2
Pistol Range	3																			3
Prison Van					2															2
Property Clerk's Office	1	9																		3
R. R. Depots and Crossings		1			6													1		11
School Census			4																	4
State Compensation		3																		1
Station House Post*		3	3	3	3	3	3	3	3	3	3	3	3	3	3	3	3	3		51
Stock Yards		1																		1
Supt. Motive Power		1																		1
Telephone Switchboard	5	1																		5
Vice Squad		1																		12
Watchman, H. D.		1																		1
Welfare Bureau																				1
White Tag Office, Summons	2																		1	3
Zoo																				1
Totals	55	30	8	10	17	4	7	9	14	11	8	4	6	14	3	3	3	4	2	212

*Our principal park is covered by Precinct Sub 17.

Seven men are required to relieve patrolmen on Station House Post for vacations.

Vice Squad—eight to thirty men are detailed to vice squad at different times, an additional seven men are required to relieve these men for vacations.

31

APPOINTMENTS

DEC.	31, '27	Captain	...............George W. McKenzie
"	31, '27	"	...............George W. Rickard
"	31, '27	"	...............Richard Cronin
"	31, '27	"	...............Charles E. Cannan
"	31, '27	"	...............Henry P. Mesner
"	31, '27	"	...............James A. Russell
"	31, '27	"	...............Joseph B. McCormick
"	31, '27	Lieutenant	...............Robert H. Stahrr
"	31, '27	"	...............Michael J. Scanlon
"	31, '27	"	...............Edwin F. Grawunder
"	31, '27	"	...............Bronislaus Panek
"	31, '27	"	...............William F. Schurpf
"	31, '27	"	...............Charles F. Wienand
"	31, '27	"	...............Patrick J. Tobin
"	31, '27	Patrolman	...............Louis P. Kirchmyer
"	31, '27	"	...............Arthur W. Lefke
"	31, '27	"	...............John M. Slattery
"	31, '27	"	...............Fred. A. Seames
"	31, '27	"	...............Thomas F. O'Neill
"	31, '27	"	...............William J. Miller
"	31, '27	"	...............George P. Green
JAN.	16, '28	Commissioner	...............James W. Higgins
"	16, '28	Dep. Commissioner	...............John S. Marnon
"	16, '28	" "	...............Frank J. Carr
JAN.	9, '28	Laborer	...............Francis A. Burke
"	13, '28	"	...............Louis Frascella
"	13, '28	"	...............Martin Wendlinger
"	22, '28	"	...............Henry Wehrum
"	22, '28	"	...............Thomas J. Collins
FEB.	6, '28	Patrolman	...............Leroy E. Fremming
"	6, '28	"	...............Edwin W. Shambaugh
"	15, '28	Laborer	...............Stephen A. Jed
"	29, '28	Patrolman	...............Joseph H. Gastle
"	29, '28	"	...............Frank A. Johnson
"	.29, '28	"	...............Everett J. Heft
"	29, '28	Janitress	...............Maude Barry
MAR.	15, '28	Patrolman	...............Fred. D. Fitch
"	15, '28	"	...............Benjamin Betz
"	26, '28	Laborer	...............Fred Ludeman
APR.	12, '28	Batteryman	...............Chester B. Kern
"	30, '28	Lieutenant	...............Oscar H. Dabritz
MAY	1, '28	Patrolman	...............Charles T. Miller
"	1, '28	"	...............Thomas C. Vogel
"	1, '28	"	...............Jeremiah G. Eberhardt
"	1, '28	"	...............Edwin J. Hoffman
"	1, '28	"	...............Herman F. Steigler
"	1, '28	"	...............Arnold E. Andres
"	1, '28	"	...............Boleslaus W. Isieja
"	10, '28	Captain	...............William Coughlin
"	10, '28	Lieutenant	...............Edmund A. Pomplum
"	23, '28	Patrolman	...............Ralph Garrett
"	23, '28	"	...............Clarence W. Hauptman
"	29, '28	Asst. Instrument Repr.	...............Francis L. Collins
JUNE	1, '28	Patrolman	...............Bonislaus W. Zamrok
"	1, '28	"	...............Julius J. Widzinski
JULY	7, '28	Temporary Lab.	...............John Gallagher
"	7, '28	" "	...............James Stanton
"	13, '28	Patrolman	...............Stanley T. Gorski
"	13, '28	"	...............Edward J. Kent
"	13, '28	"	...............Wallace J. Snell

APPOINTMENTS

"	17, '28	Desk Lieutenant	...............Richard Newell
"	19, '28	Patrolman	...............Thaddeus J. Jendrasiak
AUG.	31, '28	Captain	...............William R. Connelly
"	31, '28	Lieutenant	...............Stanley M. Szczechowiak
"	31, '28	"	...............Willard E. Ault
"	31, '28	"	...............Arthur D. Britt
"	31, '28	Patrolman	...............Fred J. Beuche
"	31, '28	"	...............Charles E. Mattison
"	31, '28	"	...............Anthony J. Schleidt
"	31, '28	"	...............Anthony B. Brock
"	31, '28	"	...............Clarence C. Hedges
SEPT.	13, '28	"	...............Henry J. Maxwell
"	13, '28	"	...............Arthur E. Amplement
"	17, '28	"	...............George N. Stein
"	27, '28	Laborer	...............Paul J. Bowen
OCT.	5, '28	Patrolman	...............Robert E. Harrington
"	5, '28	"	...............James F. R. Mack
NOV.	1, '28	Laborer	...............Martin J. Crotty
"	1, '28	Patrolman	...............James J. McMahon
"	1, '28	"	...............Leo. P. Gassman
"	1, '28	"	...............Thomas H. Cunningham
"	16, '28	Patrolman	...............Charles Van Driest
DEC.	14, '28	Patrolman	...............George J. Roob
"	17, '28	Laborer	...............Harry H. Wallmeyer
"	17, '28	"	...............James Stanton

PROMOTIONS

DEC.	31, '27	Lieut. to Captain	...............George W. McKenzie
"	31, '27	" " "	...............George W. Rickard
"	31, '27	" " "	...............Richard Cronin
"	31, '27	" " "	...............Charles E. Cannan
"	31, '27	" " "	...............Henry P. Mesner
"	31, '27	" " "	...............James A. Russell
"	31, '27	" " "	...............Joseph B. McCormick
"	31, '27	Patrolman to Lieutenant	...............Robert H. Stahrr
"	31, '27	" " "	...............Edwin F. Grawunder
"	31, '27	" " "	...............Bronislaus Panek
"	31, '27	" " "	...............William F. Schurpf
"	31, '27	" " "	...............Patrick J. Tobin
"	31, '27	Detective Sergt. to Lieut.	...............Charles F. Wienand
"	31, '27	Detective to Lieutenant	...............Michael J. Scanlon
JAN.	30, '28	Patrolman to Detective	...............William J. Murphy
FEB.	4, '28	Patrolman to Detective	...............George H. Phillips
"	4, '28	" " "	...............Ray H. Fries
APR.	30, '28	Detective to Lieutenant	...............Oscar H. Dabritz
"	30, '28	Detective to Detective Sergt.	...............James D. Johnson
"	30, '28	Patrolman to Detective	...............Guy C. Dewey
"	30, '28	" " "	...............William F. Hofmeister
"	30, '28	" " "	...............Roger Kane
MAY	10, '28	Lieutenant to Captain	...............William Coughlin
"	10, '28	Patrolman to Lieutenant	...............Edmund A. Pomplum
JULY	3, '28	Detective to Detective Sergt.	...............James Carroll
"	3, '28	Patrolman to Detective	...............Bernard M. Hofmayr
AUG.	31, '28	Lieutenant to Captain	...............William R. Connolly
"	31, '28	Patrolman to Lieutenant	...............Stanley M. Czczechowiak
"	31, '28	Patrolman to Lieutenant	...............Willard E. Ault
"	31, '28	Detective to Lieutenant	...............Arthur D. Britt
"	31, '28	Patrolman to Detective	...............Ford J. Rogers
"	31, '28	Asst. Chief of Dept. to Chief Detectives	...............John G. Reville

AUG. 31, '28 Det. Sergt. to Asst. Chief of		
	Detectives	................Thomas J. Riordan
SEPT.	6, '28 Detective to Det. Sergeant	................John T. Fagan
"	13, '28 Patrolman to Detective	...............Jeremiah J. Cronin

REINSTATED

JAN.	31 Patrolman	................Henry J. Bauman
FEB.	6 Patrolman	................Joseph S. Tyrakowski
AUG.	13 Patrolman	................Joseph R. Barrett

REDUCTIONS

AUG. 31 Chief of Detectives to Captain	................Austin J. Roche

SUPERANNUATED

MAR.	1 Patrolman	................John R. Potts
"	1 Policewoman	................Lillian Hartnett
"	1 Janitress	................Margaret Wallace
"	10 Patrolman	................Emil Emendorfer
MAY	1 Lieutenant	................William G. Jordan
"	1 Detective	................Simon J. Crotty
"	1 Patrolman	................Louis Rosenow
"	1 "	................James Mahoney
"	1 "	................William J. Kern
JUNE	1 "	................Lemuel H. Cassety
"	1 "	................Joseph B. Kirst
JULY	1 "	................William F. Conley
"	1 "	................Dennis Driscoll
"	1 "	................Henry Moriarity
AUG.	1 Captain	................Harvey J. Fogelsonger
"	6 Patrolman	................John Quinlan
"	7 Lieutenant	................George D. Richards
OCT.	1 Patrolman	................William T. Stata
"	7 "	................Louis Walter
"	7 "	................Herbert H. Baker
"	7 "	................Bart Larkin

RESIGNATIONS

JAN.	14 Laborer	................Charles F. Carney
FEB.	13 Patrolman	................Edwin W. Shambaugh
JUNE	12 Desk Lieutenant	................George W. Kinney
AUG.	7 Lieutenant	................Robert Stahrr
SEPT.	12 Patrolman	................Clarence B. Tashenberg
"	15 "	................Thomas V. Jordan
"	30 "	................Edwin J. Hoffman

DROPPED

FEB. 15 Laborer	................Dennis J. O'Leary

DISMISSALS

FEB. 23 Patrolman	................John M. McCulle

DIED

JAN.	19 Patrolman	................Edward Herrman
"	25 "	................James C. Galley
"	30 Detective	................Emil Nielsen
FEB.	2 Patrolman	................John T. Manley
APR.	7 Laborer	................Charles W. Muhlfield
"	19 Detective Sergeant	................George Maloney

APR.	27	Patrolman	................William H. Fitzgerald
MAY	5	Captain	................Francis A. Bird
"	15	Patrolman	................Michael Walsh
JUNE	26	Detective Sergeant	................John J. Kern
JULY	24	Patrolman	................John J. Sullivan
AUG.	27	Patrolman	................John Hogan
OCT.	30	Foreman of Construction	................Frank Marion
NOV.	12	Patrolman	................William J. Hyde
DEC.	3	"	................Ray C. Martin
"	23	"	................Harold Haltam

TRANSFERS

JAN. 31 Clerk from Dept. of Police to Dept.
   of Purchase   ....Leo. P. Boyle
JAN. 31 Stenog. Clerk Dept. of Police to Dept.
   of Purchase   ....William J. Cramer

CPSIA information can be obtained
at www.ICGtesting.com
Printed in the USA
BVHW050049061118
532207BV00023B/3250/P